TOUGH QUESTIONS

TOUGH QUESTIONS

answered by
LUIS PALAU

HODDER AND STOUGHTON
LONDON SYDNEY AUCKLAND TORONTO

British Library Cataloguing in Publication Data

Palau, Luis
 Tough Questions.——(Hodder Christian
 paperbacks)
 1. Christian life——1960-
 I. Title
 248.4   BV4501.2

 ISBN 0 340 35541 7

*Hodder and Stoughton Editorial Office: 47 Bedford Square, London
WC1B 3DP*

CONTENTS

1

Question: *Mr. Palau, what do you do to keep from getting bored with your wife? I have been married for ten years and, frankly, my wife bores me.*

Let me ask you a few questions before I answer yours. Are you an exciting person yourself? Are you fun to live with? Have you ever considered the possibility that *you* might be a bore?

As a husband, you can make your wife boring or interesting, nagging or charming. *You* make the difference, depending on how you treat her. So my suggestion is that you make up your mind to help your wife become attractive and interesting again through the power of love. Let me explain that in practical terms.

First, accept your wife just as she is without trying to change her. Think about when you fell in love with her, when you proposed to her, when you married her. You saw something special in her, didn't you? Now why do you find her boring ten years later? It's possible you've changed, not she. So accept your wife as the special person she is.

Then, consider the way you treat your wife. Have you surprised her from time to time with a little gift? Do you show her that you still love her, that you want to make her happy? If you have stopped doing those special things for her that you did when you were younger,

7

then you've simply become bored with yourself, not your wife. It's time to change!

Take an interest in your wife's activities rather than just your own. Discover her needs and take steps to meet them. Don't come home at night complaining about your day. Instead, ask how *her* day went. Be sure not to leave your wife at home all the time, either. Go out for dinner with her regularly. Start making plans, as well, for an exciting mini-holiday the two of you can take together soon. Go somewhere that *she* will enjoy. Be creative! There's no reason why you should stay bored – or boring.

Let me summarise all this, using the words of the Bible: 'Husbands, love your wives, just as Christ loved the church and gave himself up for her' (Eph. 5: 25). If, with God's help, you practise that kind of love, you will be on your way to a happy, exciting marriage.

Note. The most exciting marriage is formed between three people: you, your wife, and God. In chapter 29 I explain how both of you can put God at the foundation of your married life. Then pray and study the Bible together – you will see marvellous changes.

2

Question: *Mr. Palau, I have a son who has been crippled since birth. Then, a year and a half ago he lost three fingers in an accident. In spite of this, he writes well, plays and is very agile. But I think that as he grows up he will suffer psychologically because of his handicap. How can I help him?*

You say that your son's handicap hasn't prevented him from excelling in a number of physical activities. I'm glad to hear that. You haven't told me what crippled him from birth, nor how old he is, but it sounds as though he is coping well physically.

It isn't uncommon for people to compensate for their handicaps and actually surpass their peers. John Powell mentions several examples in his book, *Why Am I Afraid To Tell You Who I Am?*

Glen Cunningham, the first of the famous American mile runners, probably became such a great runner trying to strengthen his legs which were seriously crippled at age seven in a fire that almost took his life.

Charles Atlas became the first of the famous body builders because, as an adolescent, his puny physique was such an embarrassment to him.

I think you will agree with me that there is no need to be over-anxious about your son's physical condition.

But what seems to concern you the most is the possibility that he might suffer psychologically.

I appreciate your concern for your son's well-being. But you needn't worry that he will suffer psychologically because he is crippled. All of us suffer to some degree mentally or emotionally. The effects of that suffering aren't so much related to our outward physical problems as they are to our own inner strength.

'Every disadvantage has an equal or greater advantage,' someone has said. I agree. Your son's physical disadvantage could actually help him become stronger psychologically. Encourage him to excel intellectually and morally – and socially, too.

My own mother-in-law was stricken by polio at the age of 42. She has been in a wheel-chair now for more than twenty years, but she hasn't allowed her handicap to limit her personal development or interaction with others. Every Wednesday night, for instance, she serves as a girls' club leader. She has an outstanding influence for good among those girls.

History is full of examples of those who excelled despite physical limitations. Encourage your son to read about the lives of such people as Florence Nightingale (who reorganised the hospitals of England while sick in bed herself), Franklin D. Roosevelt (who led the United States to victory in the Second World War while confined to a wheel-chair), and Helen Keller (who overcame severe handicaps to become a highly respected lecturer and author).

I want to recommend one book in particular that I think both you and your son will find fascinating. It was written by a young woman, who, at the age of 18, broke her neck in a swimming accident. Now she is a quadriplegic, paralysed from the neck down.

This young woman's name is Joni Eareckson Tada, and her book is simply entitled *Joni*. In the book she honestly shows how God has helped her to overcome her personal limitations and lead an active, productive and satisfying life.

3

Question: *My mother died six years ago. Now my father is remarried, but our stepmother is very domineering and has bad habits. She isn't the least bit concerned about taking care of my younger brothers and sisters. What can I do?*

Would your father agree with your description and evaluation of his new wife? What do you think? You miss your mother and this stepmother seems like an intruder in your home. I can understand that. But is she really all bad?

It's important that you see your stepmother realistically. How? The Bible tells us, 'whatever is true, whatever is noble, whatever is right, whatever is pure, whatever is lovely, whatever is admirable – if anything is excellent or praiseworthy – think about such things' (Phil. 4: 8).

Start by writing down all the good things you see in your stepmother. Remember that she loves your father. She decided to marry him. She willingly accepted the responsibility of helping to care for you and your younger brothers and sisters. Spend at least twenty-five minutes writing down every positive thing that comes to mind about her.

If you still feel upset about your stepmother's actions and attitudes, talk to your father when the two of you can be absolutely alone. Tell him the good and the bad things you feel about his new wife. But keep your statements humble and gentle, not loud or insulting.

Remember, your father chose to marry this woman. He must love her and most likely will try to defend her. Speak respectfully about her. Ask your father for his help and advice so that you can get on better with her.

Your father will probably remind you to obey your stepmother. That advice comes directly from the Bible: 'Children, obey your parents in everything, for this pleases the Lord' (Col. 3: 20). God has given her the authority and responsibility to be your new mother, despite her imperfections. Your responsibility is to obey her.

When your real mother died, you were forced as a young girl to step into her shoes. That meant doing a lot of growing up quickly, didn't it? But now that your father has remarried, you need to step out of those shoes and let your stepmother fill them. That won't be easy, but it's essential for the welfare of your family.

If your stepmother refuses to take proper care of your younger brothers and sisters, you may need to help again from time to time. Be sure to talk to your father first about this. Before God, *he* is ultimately responsible for his children, not you.

Whatever your stepmother does, love her by your positive behaviour. Help look after your brothers and sisters, when needed, without complaining. Obey her willingly in love, not begrudgingly. Your stepmother may change, and you'll certainly become a better person if you accept her as she is and show her love.

4

Question: Mr. Palau, I'd like to know whether you think children should obey their parents no matter what they ask. Can it be possible that just because they are parents they never make mistakes?

You're obviously not a young child from the way your letter is worded. You don't give your exact age, but I assume you're a teenager. Is that sarcasm I sense in your questions? Of course, my answer to whether 'they never make mistakes' is 'No.'

But, your letter does put me on the spot. As the father of four boys, I know I've made my share of mistakes. One incident that occurred several years ago comes to mind.

I was getting ready before a trip and becoming more frustrated every minute. The boys still weren't in bed, my suit-cases weren't packed, and it was getting late! It was my own fault, but the whole family had to suffer with me. When I finally went to bed that night, I found a little note on my pillow. This is what it said:

Dad is mad. I am sad. I'm not glad 'cause Dad is mad. So, Lord, change Dad.

It was signed by all four boys. That humbled me. I went to every bed and hugged my boys and kissed them and asked for their forgiveness.

Parents *do* make mistakes. We're not perfect. But let me give you several practical reasons why young people should respect and obey their parents.

First your parents have more experience than you. We all generally improve our performance as we gain more experience. That's true whether we're learning to swim, drive, or make wise decisions about our friendships. Respect your parents for the experience they have accumulated over the years.

Second, most likely your parents genuinely love you and want the best for your life. Sometimes it may not seem like that when they impose certain rules and restrictions. But remember that they know you well and want to help you in the best way possible.

Third, your parents may want to help you avoid some of the mistakes they made. They may not always tell you about the foolish things they did when they were younger. But inwardly they are thinking, 'I remember making a mistake when I went to that certain place or did that particular thing. I don't want my son or daughter to go through the same heartache by repeating that mistake.'

Let me add one more important reason why you should obey and respect your parents. God promises to bless your life if you do. He says to each of us: 'Children, obey your parents in the Lord, for this is right. "Honour your father and mother" – which is the first commandment with a promise – "that it may go well with you and that you may enjoy long life on the earth"' (Eph. 6: 1-3). If you honour your parents, the hand of God will be upon your life for good.

Now you may be saying, 'Hey, Luis, I don't even believe in God. Who cares what the Bible says, anyway?' Listen, whether you believe in God or not is not the point. God is alive. He created you and He has set down the rules for a successful life. Whether you're flying a plane, playing football or running a race, if you follow the rules you'll succeed. You'll become a winner in the long run.

There does come a point, however, when you should *disobey* your parents. The crucial exception to the rule is when your parents ask you to do something that is morally wrong. I read a report recently which said that half of the runaway children leave home because their parents subject them to incest, mistreatment and brutality. It breaks my heart to think that parents could do such things.

So what should you do if your parents ask you to do something immoral? First, explain to them why you can't do what they say. Don't act rebelliously. Simply state how you feel about the action they want you to take.

Next, if your parents refuse to reason with you, then tell them, 'I'm going to have to talk to someone about this.' As soon as possible, contact an adult you can trust and tell them what is happening in your home. I recommend talking to a minister and his wife, if possible.

Finally, talk to God Himself about your parents. Even if you haven't prayed for ten years, start now. He can change your parents. Because He loves you, He wants to help you to get on with them.

5

Question: *Three months ago I started going out with Dave. The problem is that wherever we go, he always wants a drink but not just one. He goes on until he is sick. What can I do to help him?*

Your friend may not be an alcoholic yet. He's probably just drinking for the thrills – and maybe to impress you. If you want to impress *him*, stop going out with him. You might shake him out of his drinking habit and spare him from a life of misery. And think about your own future. As a young woman, you have most of your life ahead of you. Why get stuck with a loser?

It's not going to be easy to end your relationship with Dave, but think of the consequences if you don't. Listen to what others have told me after realising what alcohol was doing to their marriages:

I have a problem with alcohol. I started drinking when I was quite young. I lost quite a few jobs and ended up in the gutter. Now I'm married, but I'm scared that I am going right back down into the gutter again.

I was married twenty-five years ago and have seven children. My husband is a drunken, adulterous and cruel man who often beats me. A month ago he took off without leaving us any money.

I'm a hopeless drunk. I can't stop drinking. I have

17

eight children, and when I drink I hit them without knowing what I'm doing. My wife wants to leave me because I beat her, too.

Sounds as though they lived happily ever after, doesn't it? Don't believe the fairy tale that Dave is going to get any better once you get married.

May I remind you what God says about your situation? His Word declares, 'Wine is a mocker and beer a brawler; whoever is led astray by them is not wise' (Prov. 20: 1). Don't let Dave's drinking habits make a fool of you.

After you stop seeing Dave, start thinking about the type of young man you want to marry eventually. Remember, be choosy – don't rush to marry the first man that comes along.

When you meet a young man who interests you, ask yourself several questions, such as: How does he get on with his family? With my family? In what ways does he treat me with respect? How will he treat me after we're married? How committed is he to wait until marriage before experiencing sexual intimacy? Does he have any habits that annoy others? Is he willing to change them? Is he a consistent, productive worker? Has he committed his life totally to God? Will he be a godly, spiritual leader in the home?

Also start thinking about the type of woman you want to become. Instead of focusing all your attention on *finding* the right person, decide to *become* the right person. Develop those qualities which will make you attractive to the best young men.

I am not just talking about physical attraction. There is more to you than how you look. Develop spiritual qualities like purity, gentleness, kindness and wisdom. (See Proverbs 31: 10-31 for a more complete list.)

My wife, Pat, has discovered the secret of becoming a beautiful woman. We've been married for more than twenty years, and I think she's getting more beautiful every day! Why? Because she doesn't just love me – she

18

has developed a deep love for God. Before you find yourself in love with some man, fall in love with God. Then make sure that anybody you make a date with also loves God with all his heart, soul, mind and strength (Deut. 6: 5; Mark 12: 30).

Why settle for a potentially disastrous relationship with a loser like Dave? No matter how much you feel for him, think! Stop seeing him and trust God for the best. You'll be the winner in the long run.

6

Question: *I have some pretty big doubts about Christianity. It doesn't make sense to me that everyone is 'lost' if they don't receive Jesus Christ as Saviour. If I had been born in India or China or Saudi Arabia, I probably would have accepted the religion of the country. Why should Christianity alone be true? All other religions have people who believe fervently that they are right.*

Your letter expresses a question that many people are asking today: What right do Christians have to claim that Christ is the only way to heaven? For centuries Britain was considered a 'Christian' country. But that's no longer true, as a large number of adherents to Hinduism, Islam and other religions have made their homes here. So it's natural to wonder, 'Aren't these other religions valid, too?'

I appreciate the fact that you have taken the time to write me. Of course, I shall be somewhat biased in answering your question. So would a Moslem friend be if you asked him about the claims of Islam. As a Christian, I have come to realise that it's not a man-made religion that we need, but a God-given revelation. That's one of the reasons that Christianity is different from any other religion. It is God's revelation of Himself through His Son, Jesus Christ.

I do believe that Christianity alone is true. That doesn't mean I'm prejudiced or look down on other religions. I simply have come to the conclusion that Christianity alone has the ring of authenticity.

Oh, I commend those who sincerely believe this or that religion. But is sincerity enough?

You begin your letter by making two subjective statements. First, you say that Christianity alone being true doesn't make sense to you. Second, you contend that that possibility doesn't seem fair to those born in traditionally non-Christian nations.

You then develop an objective argument against Christianity alone being true. Let us examine this argument in more detail.

Major premise: All religions have sincere followers (who believe their religion is true).

Minor premise: All religions which have sincere followers are true.

Conclusion: Thus, all religions are true (not just Christianity).

Your major premise that all religions have sincere followers is a correct observation. Any respectable animist sincerely believes he must seek to appease the evil spirits around him. Any practising Moslem sincerely believes he must pray five times a day towards Mecca. And any self-proclaimed atheist sincerely believes that both the animists and the Moslems are fools. So you're right, every religious persuasion does have followers who sincerely believe that their particular religion is right.

But is your minor premise that all religions are true if they have sincere followers also correct? 'Sincerity' and 'fervently believe' are emotional terms. 'No matter what you say, I sincerely believe I'm right!' But feelings don't always correspond to reality. History records the atrocities and follies of many people who were sincerely *wrong*.

The truth-value of any religion or belief must be evaluated by the cornerstone of every system of logic: A is not non-A. If you compared each tenet of one religion with the corresponding tenets of other religions, you would find many conflicting ideas.

Suppose you had grown up in India, you probably would be inclined to worship a host of idols. But if you had grown up in Saudi Arabia you would be horrified to think that anyone could believe in any other god than Allah. And if you grew up in communist China, you probably wouldn't believe in any gods at all.

Now, everybody *can't* be right! If Islam is right when it claims that Allah alone is God, then logically we must conclude that Hinduism and atheism *must* be false. Thus, since all religions deny some of the basic tenets of all other faiths, only one religion at best can be true. All religions contain *some* truth, but virtually all contain errors as well.

No matter which particular religion is actually true, assuming one is right, it wouldn't be 'fair' to the millions of people who live in areas of the world where that religion isn't accepted or practised. Suppose Buddhism was the one true religion. That wouldn't be fair to the Australians, would it? But to whom are you going to complain?

If a small boat capsizes in the English Channel and only one person survives – because he was the only one who knew how to swim – whose fault is that? You certainly couldn't scowl at the survivor. Wouldn't you agree, though it's a bit late for our hypothetical friends, that it would have been best if they had all learned how to swim before the accident?

Similarly, wouldn't you also agree that it would be best if every person accepted personal responsibility for his own beliefs? If the beliefs you were taught don't correspond to reality, then *you* need carefully to examine the claims of the other major religions of the world. You certainly don't want to believe something that's wrong when eternity is at stake.

If you honestly want to find the truth and base your way of life on it, then try this strategy suggested by John Stott. He has spent considerable time discussing the claims of various religions with university students and others. He recommends that any spiritual search should begin by trying to communicate with the One who created the heavens and earth, and saying:

> *God, if You exist – and I don't know that You do, and if You can hear this prayer, and I don't know if You can – I want to tell You that I am an honest seeker after truth. Show me if Jesus is Your Son and the only Saviour of the world. And if You bring conviction to my mind, I will trust Him as my Saviour. I will follow Him as my Master and I will obey Him as the King of my life.*

You say you have some big doubts about Christianity. Perhaps it's not true after all. Perhaps it is. Find out by examining its claims as recorded in the New Testament. Begin reading at the Gospel of Luke, using a modern-language version of the Bible.

If Christianity isn't true, we both have much searching ahead. But don't accept Christianity just because I happen to believe it or because a friend of yours gives lip-service to it. Pursue the treasure we call truth until you find it, and then share it with everyone you meet. I'm looking forward to hearing what you find out.

7

Question: *I'm 14 years old and I have two brothers and a sister. My problem is that I don't get along with my mum very well. I try to get along, but I can't. We shout and argue a lot. I don't know what to do.*

First of all, I wish you would ask your mother to write to me. I'd like to be able to correspond with her. Many parents today feel frustrated because their children don't get along with them. So I should like to hear your mother's views on the problem you describe. Remember, 'The first to present his case seems right, till another comes forward and questions him' (Prov. 18: 17).

Second, have you ever talked to your father about this problem? You don't even mention him in your letter. I have an idea he may have abandoned you and your mother. If your mum and dad are divorced or separated, tell him about your problem the next time you see him. He may be able to give you some advice.

Third, when you sense an argument starting between you and your mother, quietly excuse yourself and go to your room. Close the door and say to God, 'I need your help.' Then count slowly to twenty and cool off instead of shouting and arguing with her. The Bible says, 'A hot-tempered man stirs up dissension, but a patient man calms a quarrel' (Prov. 15: 18).

Fourth, try to understand the pressures your mother

is facing. I assume by your letter she is bringing up you and your sister and two brothers by herself. My mother found herself alone when I was only ten years old. My father didn't divorce her; he died. It wasn't until I was older that I realised how lonely my mother felt.

You probably haven't realised what a lonely task it is for your mother to raise four children by herself. From the picture I get in your letter, she probably goes out to work. She may feel terribly frustrated, tired and lonely. Seek to encourage her, and not to argue with her.

Fifth, follow the advice of the greatest psychotherapist of all time. On several occasions He told people, 'Honour your father and mother.' Who is this well-known psychotherapist? It's God Himself. Even though you're only 14 years old, God knows you, God loves you and God has His eye upon you. That's why your letter came to me in the first place. I'm not even sure how you found out my name and address, but I want to tell you this. God commands you to honour your parents and to obey them.

Have you ever considered how much you owe your parents? You owe them your very life. You owe them the clothes you wear, the food you eat, the place you sleep. They deserve your respect. Do your actions honour them when you're at school, around the neighbourhood or in the house?

Honouring your parents is an attitude of the heart. It's a question of your will. Are you willing to be obedient and submissive? Do you want to please your mother? Do you want to please your father (wherever he is)? Are you a blessing to them?

My wife, Pat, and I thank God for our four sons. They have been such a blessing to us! Andrew, for example, almost always walks into the house with a smile and a cheerful, 'Hello everybody!' He brings us happiness and cheer. You could be a joy to your mother and father by trying to be pleasant.

Especially if your dad is gone, bless your mum by doing *more* than your share of the work around the house. Before she feels tired and worn out, step in and help her. Stop arguing with her. Instead, spread a little cheerfulness around the place!

8

Question: *My husband left me and our 13-year-old daughter. He lives with another woman near our home. Should I go after him or wait to see if he comes back? He wants our daughter to live with him. Should I let her go? Please answer me.*

Should you go after your husband or not? Actually, one option is not definitely better than the other. You may rightfully decide to wait until your husband comes back to you – humbling himself, asking for your forgiveness and changing his behaviour. But before you take him back, insist that he *completely* breaks off his relationship with the other woman, and shows what the Bible calls 'fruit in keeping with repentance' (Luke 3: 8).

On the other hand, you can try to reason with your estranged husband. If he truly loves his daughter, then his responsibility as a father is to return to your home. But if he decides to come back, as I said before, he must repent of his adultery and honestly want to restore and strengthen your marriage.

If your husband does come back to live with you and your daughter, you will all find the transition difficult for a while. The old problems are likely to flare up again. Experience shows that a couple will repeat their past problems unless one or both of them change. That's why it's important that you also examine your heart and seek to become a better wife to him.

Please don't misunderstand me. Your husband is clearly at fault for committing adultery and leaving his family. Ignore anyone who would try to blame *you* for *his* immorality. But since you are the one who wrote, we must begin with you. So I challenge you to search your heart because if your husband does come back, you may have several areas in your life that you will need to straighten out, too.

Now, should you allow your daughter to live with your husband and his girlfriend? Definitely not!

Your husband forfeited his authority in the home when he left to live in immorality. It wouldn't be wise for you to let your daughter go to live with him at this time. His poor example could have a harmful influence on her. If he wants to see his daughter, he should visit her where she lives – at your home.

During this time when your husband has abandoned you and your daughter, do not despair. I realise that your husband has caused your family to experience much shame and grief. But remember that God promises to take special care of the abandoned. In the Old Testament we read, 'For your Maker is your husband – the Lord Almighty is His name' (Isa. 54: 5). God wants to be your husband, as it were, in this time of need. Count on it – God promises never to forsake you.

9

Question: *Mr. Palau, I am 15 years old. My parents don't get on with each other. My mother recently took driving lessons and now she is having an affair with her driving instructor. The other day he invited my mother and me to his house for a while. My mother was holding his hand. She even kissed him in my presence. My father doesn't know a thing about it.*

Do you think this relationship between my mother and this man is all right? It bothers me, but I can't say anything to my mother because she would get mad and it wouldn't do any good.

I really feel for you in the incredibly difficult situation in which your mother has put you. I can't believe that she would show affection to her driving instructor in your presence.

I sense you are torn between your mother and your father. Let's talk about your mother first. Her relationship with this other man is definitely *not* all right. The potential results of her actions are incredible. Now that's not just what I say. God's instruction book for living – the Bible – seeks to protect us from such devastating situations. It says, 'Marriage should be honoured by all, and the marriage bed kept pure, for

God will judge the adulterer and all the sexually immoral' (Heb. 13: 4).

Why does God say that? To keep us from enjoying life to the full? Not at all! In His infinite love and wisdom, He gives us this strong warning to protect us from the scars of immorality.

Your mother's actions have not only hurt you, but your whole family. You *should* talk to her. Do it with love and humility. Remember, she is your mother. Be frank, but keep your voice calm and your attitude humble.

Your mother may respond very angrily. She will probably remind you that her marriage with your father isn't going well. She may start justifying her actions and telling you why she should have this affair. Whatever she says, don't try to argue with her.

As a teenager, seek to learn from this tragic situation. First, keep yourself pure before marriage. I realise this isn't popular advice today. According to a survey conducted by National Opinion Polls, 94 per cent. of the young men and women in Britain today lose their virginity by the age of 21. But listen to what Donna, a young woman from Leicester, says:

'The first time I had sex, I was 16 and I hated it. It wasn't the way I'd imagined it would be. My mum told me that sex was wonderful if it was with the right person and I thought, "Oh, this is going to be fantastic." Well, it wasn't. I felt disgusted with myself.'

Sex before marriage carries a high price. Carefully consider its costs.

Second, marry the right young man. Don't rush into marriage. I believe the two greatest decisions in life are, in this order: What am I going to do with God and who am I going to marry? It is better to remain single if you must, than to marry the wrong sort of person.

Sarah's testimony below reflects some of the heartache that wrong choices in the areas of sex and marriage bring:

'If I had my time over again, I wouldn't have married

so soon. Not many of my friends are already married with babies – and I feel very envious of them sometimes. One girl I know has a Porsche, and what have I got? A baby and this cramped little flat and no money – just the £13.30 a week I get from supplementary benefit . . .

'Andy and I met at school and we got married when I was 16 because I was pregnant. I'll never forget the panic. Andy was in Cyprus and I was living at home with my dad and I didn't dare tell him. My parents separated when I was 11 and I just didn't know where to turn.'

Sarah went on to say: 'I hope Andy and I will stay together, though being a soldier he's away a lot, and I get bored being stuck at home all day, so perhaps one day we'll split up. The thing is you have to try so hard to make marriage work and divorce is so easy.'

Finally, remain faithful after marriage – even if the easy thing is to do just the opposite. You know what heartache your mother's unfaithfulness has already caused. That pain will only intensify if she eventually divorces your father. Don't repeat her mistakes.

10

Question: *Mr. Palau, I am a 20-year-old man. I have a girlfriend who is 17. She has been hinting that she wants a family and wants to get married. I am unemployed at present, but she doesn't understand that. She's rather hasty and she wants to marry me now.*

I'm glad you wrote to me because so many young people rush into marriage without a second thought. I'm glad you're seeking advice about this important decision. Of course, you will also want to talk this over with your parents.

I don't know either of you personally, so I can't evaluate your maturity. Some people are ready for the responsibilities of marriage at an earlier age than others. There is no 'right' age. Wisdom says, however, 'Think hard before you make such a crucial decision.'

Try to discern your motives for wanting to get married. Do you really love your girlfriend? Do you want the very best for her? Is it best for you to get married now?

Remember that love is willing to wait. It isn't based solely on our emotions and feelings, which tend to be impulsive. Love is also intelligent, wise and open-eyed. It doesn't make blind choices.

Perhaps the Song of Love says it best:

Love is very patient and kind, never jealous or

envious, never boastful or proud, never haughty or selfish or rude. Love does not demand its own way. It is not irritable or touchy. It does not hold grudges and will hardly even notice when others do it wrong. It is never glad about injustice, but rejoices whenever truth wins. If you love someone, you will be loyal to him no matter what the cost. You will always believe in him, always expect the best of him, and always stand your ground in defending him . . . Love goes on for ever.

If you want to read the entire Song of Love, you will find it in the Bible. Turn to 1 Corinthians in the New Testament, chapter 13. If you don't have a Bible, I encourage you to buy one and read a chapter every day. (I quoted from *The Living Bible*. But also consider buying *The New International Version* or a similar modern language translation.)

The Bible has more to say about love, marriage and sex than you realise! But you won't find a specific verse from God that says, 'You should get married two months from now to your girlfriend.' Instead, you will find basic truths that will help you to make wise decisions about marriage and other important matters.

Personally, I agree with you that it seems best in your case to wait before you and your girlfriend marry. Take the time to learn, to mature, to work and to become better established financially. You're both young – so what's the rush to get married?

Whenever your wedding-day is to be, decide to enter marriage pure and clean. One popular song says, 'Let's get physical.' That's exactly what you should *not* do. The world says, 'Live together and find out if you're meant for each other.' Don't fall for that either.

You and I both know individuals who have wrecked their lives because they broke God's commandments and now they're paying for it physically, mentally, emotionally and spiritually. God isn't punishing them, necessarily. They are suffering the *natural* consequences of their actions.

God is not some old grandfather in the sky who gets upset any time someone on earth starts having fun. Erase that caricature from your thinking. God is infinitely wise and good. That's why He says, 'Flee from sexual immorality.' (1 Cor. 6: 18).

Premarital sex is a very serious sin. You should avoid it, not because God might punish you, but because God is holy and He knows what harm that sin will have on you both now and later when you do marry. He wants you to remain sexually pure before marriage for your own good.

I could say much more, but I want to close by reminding you that marriage should be a triangle – one man, one woman, and God. Don't enter marriage until both you and your girlfriend know the One who can help you enjoy a happy marriage for a lifetime.

11

Question: *I often feel spiritually and physically weak. I'm almost enslaved by my nerves. At times, everything irritates me. It's not because my marriage is bad. During our four years of marriage we've never had any problems nor anything that threatens our happiness. I don't want to go to a doctor because I've lost confidence in them. But what can I do?*

Our nerves don't bother us without reason. They respond when something isn't going right in our lives – physically, emotionally or spiritually. Since you haven't told me when and under what particular circumstances you started experiencing these nervous problems, I shall keep my remarks more general. I do gather from other parts of your letter, however, that you have made a commitment to Jesus Christ.

So, first, don't disregard the help of a good doctor. Your problem could have an organic origin. You need to see a doctor, even if you say you have lost confidence in him. Don't go to him, however, just to ask for tranquillisers to mask your condition. Ask for a thorough physical examination, which may locate the source of your nervous problems.

Second, be honest with yourself. Is there unresolved guilt in your life? Are you bitter against someone? Are you angry about something or someone? Are you seeking revenge against another person? Are you worrying about becoming pregnant or about a child that isn't well or the fact that you may be unable to have children? Don't repress these things. They will only trouble your nerves more.

Third, take care of yourself physically. Get plenty of rest every night to renew your strength. Also make time to exercise daily. I find that walking calms my nerves. Try walking and other exercises and discover which help you to relax the most.

Fourth, set aside some time each day to be alone and talk to God. When everybody is gone or the little children are taking a nap while your husband is at work, take time to be alone for half an hour with God. Many people, including myself, have found great comfort and strength by reading the Psalms of David in the Old Testament. Lately I have been memorising Psalm 34. Verse 4 has encouraged me: ' I sought the Lord, and he answered me; he delivered me from all my fears.' Try reading one psalm each day. You'll find them near the middle of your family bible.

Finally, make a list of all the things that worry you and tell God about them. Ask for His strength and peace. I don't know of anything else that will calm your nerves more than to spend time alone with the Lord each day.

12

Question: *My parents died a number of years ago, and I inherited their business, which I have tried hard to maintain. In spite of all my hard work, it has gone downhill and I have lost almost everything. I need your help.*

As a young woman, you not only had to accept your parents' death but assume their responsibilities as well. You have been put in a difficult position, haven't you?

My own father died when I was young, following a brief, severe illness. When he was gone, my mother – who was only 35 at the time – found herself solely responsible for six children and a large, prospering construction business. Within three years she only had to worry about my siblings and me – the business was gone. We had nothing left but debts – lots of them.

My mother wasn't the right person to run my father's business. She was a good mother, but she knew practically nothing about running a business. She tried hard to keep the company solvent, but sometimes hard work isn't enough.

You have also tried diligently to maintain the business you inherited. Despite your efforts, it has gone almost bankrupt. Are you the right person to run this company all by yourself? The Bible says, 'Do not think of yourself more highly than you ought, but rather think of yourself with sober judgment' (Rom. 12: 3).

You may need to disband the business before you not

only lose everything but sustain debts you'll spend years repaying. It may be better to find a job somewhere else than to suffer financial ruin trying to keep a sinking ship afloat. But I'm not in the best position, honestly, to evaluate your overall financial situation – especially from the brief letter you sent me. I appreciate the fact that you have written, but are you asking the right person for advice?

If you need help with a moral or spiritual problem, or a difficult home life, then contact a Christian leader. If you need help with your car, call a reliable mechanic. If you need financial advice, contact an ethical, successful businessman whose counsel you respect and trust.

Having said that, let me share several financial principles from a man who is famous for his sound advice on the business of life – King Solomon.

Solomon was known as the wealthiest, wisest man of his day. His reign – characterised by peace and prosperity – marked the zenith of history in the Middle East. Today thousands of people still profit from reading his book of Proverbs – considered to be some of the most practical advice ever penned. Here are some of the general principles you will find in that short book about working and operating a business.

First, whatever you do – do it diligently. Solomon would have commended you for your hard work. He says, 'Lazy hands make a man poor, but diligent hands bring wealth' (Prov. 10:4). But diligence isn't enough, as you've learned.

Second, pursue sound business ventures. Seeking quick wealth or easy money is foolish. Solomon states, 'He who works his land will have abundant food, but he who chases fantasies lacks judgment' (12: 11). On another occasion he reiterates, 'He who works his land will have abundant food, but the one who chases fantasies will have his fill of poverty' (28: 19).

Third, continue to improve your skills in order to become proficient in your vocation. Yesterday's skills are tomorrow's liabilities. Keep up to date on the advances in your line of work. Solomon notes, 'Do you see a man skilled in his work? He will serve before kings; he will not serve obscure men' (22: 29).

Fourth, carefully oversee your financial matters. As you have discovered, wealth can disappear if not managed well. Solomon advises, 'Be sure you know the condition of your flocks, give careful attention to your herds; for riches do not endure for ever' (27: 23–4).

Finally, consult business professionals who can help you avoid foolish mistakes and thus make wise decisions. Solomon adds, 'Plans fail for lack of counsel, but with many advisers they succeed' (15:22). You should have started doing this years ago, but maybe it's not too late yet. You might be able to revive your parents' business with the help of several competent financial advisers. But even if you have to start again, the principles above will help you to succeed in whatever you do. I wish you the best of good fortune.

13

Question: *I have a 15-year-old son who makes life impossible for me. He wants to stop going to school and spends his time running around in the streets with his friends until late at night.*

My husband is a good man, but he doesn't like to argue with our son. He suffers in silence, but I can't tolerate the situation any more. I live in constant tension. What can I do?

Let's talk about your husband first. I hope he's reading this letter, by the way. You imply in other parts of your letter that your husband lacks authority in the home. I get the impression he is a weak, ineffectual man who needs to start acting like a man around the house.

To begin with, your husband should have dealt with your son's misbehaviour years ago. Instead, he has chosen to 'suffer in silence'. But who does he think he is deceiving? *You* are suffering the consequences of his failure to stop your teenage son from doing as he pleases. Nobody wins when a man loses his courage to be the kind of husband and father God intended him to be.

Your husband needs to sit down with your son and confront him with his disrespectful behaviour. It sounds as though your husband has never instructed your son in the ways of the Lord. The Bible says, 'These commands that I give you today are to be upon your hearts. Impress them on your children. Talk about them when you sit at home and when you walk along the road, when you lie down and when you get up' (Deut. 6: 6-7).

But your husband has shirked his responsibility by saying he doesn't like to argue with his son. Argue? Whoever said a father was supposed to argue with his son?

But he should start communicating with your son on an adult level, man to man.

First, your husband – with your support – must tell your son that *he* is responsible for his own actions. I realise that isn't a popular idea today. Dr. John Bruce, a noted sociologist, comments: 'For a long time, the principal currency has been that somehow, children aren't responsible for their own actions. They are the product of poor upbringing, inappropriate role models, bad teachers, the socio-economic system, heaven knows what.

'Let's assume for a moment that all these things might be true. That means children that aren't responsible moral agents. Yet eventually, they will have to accept responsibility.'

What your son needs to realise is that he *is* a responsible moral person. No matter how well or how poorly you have raised him, no matter how wealthy or how poverty-stricken you may be, he is accountable to God, to society and to you as his parents – particularly as long as he lives at home – for his behaviour.

Second, as parents you should teach your son that he must bear the consequences of his actions. Don't allow your teenager to assume that if he leaves school or runs around with his late-night friends that you're going to bail him out when he gets in trouble. 'The parent who is too quick to bail his child out of difficulty may be doing him a disservice,' according to Dr. James Dobson, noted marriage and family counsellor.

Dobson goes on to explain: 'We sometimes keep our

children from coming to their senses by preventing them from feeling the consequences of their own mistakes. When a teenager gets a speeding ticket, *he* should pay for it. When he wrecks his car, *he* should have it fixed. When he gets suspended from school, *he* should take the consequences.'

Third, you and your husband need to discipline your son when he steps out of line. Frankly, it's almost too late in your case. This problem didn't start overnight – it's developed over the years. Your son is already 15 and will be going out on his own soon. But as long as he lives in your home, he has no right to talk back to you, drop out of school or stay out late at night against your wishes. When he disobeys, he should be disciplined.

By discipline I *don't* mean punishment. Punishment is an act administered for the welfare of the group (whether that group is society in general or the family in particular). Discipline, on the other hand, is a relationship fostered for the welfare of a particular individual (in this case, your son). If you really love your son and care about his welfare, you will discipline him.

In the book of Proverbs we read, 'He who spares the rod hates his son, but he who loves him is careful to discipline him' (13: 24). Proverbs also says, 'The rod of correction imparts wisdom, but a child left to itself disgraces his mother' (29: 15). The longer you refuse to discipline your son, the more he will cause you grief.

Your son may threaten to rebel if you and your husband start disciplining him in love. But in the long run, I believe he will respect you and become a more mature young man for it. Deep inside, he wants limits and boundaries. But remember, discipline is a *relationship*, not an act. First seek to demonstrate love, develop rapport and set aside time for your son. Once he knows you care about him discipline will be possible.

If you have failed your son in any way, pinpoint that failure and ask your son to forgive you. Humble yourself and admit to him that you make mistakes, too.

Your attempts to discipline your son will be hypocritical unless you have become transparent before him.

Is discipline really necessary? Yes! It's never out of date. An army without discipline will be defeated. A home without discipline will be destroyed. Discipline may not be pleasant, but it's vital.

Your son has made life impossible for you. Your husband has permitted it. It's going to take an act of God to change your family – literally. I've told you what I believe God's Word teaches. But read it for yourself. I would recommend as a couple – and even as an entire family if possible – that you read one chapter from the book of Proverbs each day.

God wants to revolutionise your home. I challenge you to let Him.

14

Question: *My wife is very sick. She has cancer. I'd like to know what would happen if after all these months of abstention I had sexual relations with another woman. Would it be all that wrong?*

Your dilemma is not unique. Many people face periods during their marriage – whether due to work, pregnancy or illness – where normal sexual relationships are interrupted. With that abstention comes the sexual temptation to seek release and pleasure outside marriage.

No doubt, you feel that temptation strongly. Apparently you want to rationalise giving in to it. But consider that when you married, you promised to remain faithful to your wife in poverty and in wealth, in sickness and in health, until death separated you. You made a commitment and a vow to her. Are you a man of your word or not?

What would you think if your wife decided, for some reason, to be unfaithful to you? How would you feel? Don't fool yourself – you would feel jealous and probably angry.

The *Daily Mail* recently discussed a study conducted by Dr. Annette Lawson, a sociology lecturer at Brunel University. Dr. Lawson, who questioned 700 people in her research, found that infidelity is more destructive to marriage than ever, even though many men and women no longer consider it wrong.

Adultery is a sin, no matter how many people say it's not. From ancient times one of the basic tenets of morality has been, 'You shall not commit adultery' (Exod. 20: 14). It's never right to do wrong.

If you deceive your wife, you will deeply hurt her – and yourself. You risk losing your peace, your sense of self-esteem and your marriage. That's a high price to pay over a lifetime for one moment of passion, wouldn't you say?

My own wife has had cancer. For a while we weren't sure how long she would live. She underwent radical surgery in an attempt to stop the spread of cancer in her body. Yes, at times we haven't been able to enjoy intimacy because of her illness or my travels. But God has given us the strength to resist the temptations that come.

Commit your own life to God and ask Him to give you the strength you need. Then let Him channel your energy towards showing love and concern for your wife during this difficult time in her life.

15

Question: *My wife walked out on me about eighteen weeks ago, and has gone to live with her mother. She refuses to talk to me on the phone. I know she's unhappy and I am very lonely. I know I have made many mistakes. How do I bridge the gap between us?*

Your wife has walked out on you and you're both miserable. Is this the end of your marriage? It doesn't have to be. I believe this particular separation might be the *best* thing that's happened to your marriage yet. Let me explain what I mean.

Though a separation is never pleasant, at least your wife has not acted disloyally or immorally by moving in with another man. Be thankful for that. She didn't move in with your mother-in-law, however, for the fun of it. So what compelled her to walk out on you?

This time of separation has forced you to admit, 'I know I have made many mistakes.' Congratulations! You have found the secret for *starting* to bridge the gap between yourself and your wife. By accepting responsibility for your 'mistakes', you will be able to win her confidence and begin to become the man she wants and needs.

'Mistakes' isn't the best word to describe what you've done, and not done, so far in your marriage, though. Most wives don't walk out on their husbands as your wife did unless they have been pushed to the brink.

How about admitting your *sins*?

The Bible tells us, 'He who conceals his sins does not prosper, but whoever confesses and renounces them finds mercy' (Prov. 28: 13).

I suggest that you spend as much time as possible today writing down all the ways you have hurt your relationship with your wife. Don't stop until you've identified all the major areas where you have failed to be the husband you should be. Then ring your wife and ask if you can meet her as soon as possible.

When you talk to your wife, don't try to justify your past actions or minimise them. Acknowledge what you have done and say, 'I know I have hurt you deeply. I don't deserve it, but will you forgive me for what I have done?'

If your wife does not even want to come to the phone to talk to you, then try a different approach. Talk to your mother-in-law! After all, your wife went back to her and has told her about your marital problems. Your mother-in-law may be bitter at the things you've done to her daughter, but she may also be eager to see the two of you back together again.

Not only have you hurt your wife, you see, but you've hurt her family. So admit to your mother-in-law: 'I haven't been the husband I promised I would be to your daughter. I have failed her – and you – in many ways. I don't deserve it, but will you forgive me for how I've treated your daughter?'

Once your mother-in-law senses your repentant attitude, she may encourage your wife to talk to you and meet you to work towards a reconciliation. Then you will need to ask for your wife's forgiveness, too.

Your marriage won't be revolutionised solely by asking for your wife's forgiveness. Let's face it. What you need to do is to start all over again. Jesus put it this way: 'You should not be surprised at my saying, "You must be born again"' (John 3: 7). Read that entire chapter in the Gospel of John to discover how you can start your life – and your marriage – anew by making a commitment to the One who invented marriage in the first place.

16

Question: *My father passed away a year ago. I knew about it because someone called to tell me. I didn't say anything about it to my mother because I didn't want her to suffer, so I lied to her.*

But my mother soon learned the truth and she says she'll never forgive me for lying to her. I'm at my wits' end. Every night I cry and can't sleep. I feel guilty about the whole situation. My mother drinks a lot now. Please, Mr. Palau, I need your advice.

As a young woman, you had good intentions. You lied to your mother to protect her from unpleasant news. Instead, besides losing your father, you also alienated your mother. Now she's drowning herself in alcohol and blaming you for her problems.

Good intentions aren't good enough, are they? I sympathise with you, since I can still remember how much my own father's death affected my mother. I sense that you were sincere in your actions. But good intentions must be coupled with right actions. Lying to your mother was the wrong thing to do.

Sir Francis Bacon wrote, 'Man prefers to believe what he prefers to be true.' Isn't that often the case? We lie to God, to others – even to ourselves – because the truth seems too painful at times. But truth never hurts unless it ought to.

One of our basic needs as humans is to know the truth. Your mother needed to know about your father's death. Were they separated or divorced at the time he died? Did you actually expect to hide his death from your mother?

Whoever called you first instead of your mother put you in an awkward and unnecessary situation. Perhaps you weren't the best person to tell her about your father's death, but you shouldn't have lied to her.

Lying is denying. It's denying the truth because we think that it will somehow go away. It won't. A lie never resolves anything. One lie leads to another and the vicious circle never stops until it eventually explodes in your face.

The Bible recognises this and commands, 'Stop lying to each other; tell the truth' (Eph. 4: 25, *The Living Bible*). Jesus Christ could say, 'I am the way and the truth and the life' (John 14: 6). But our natural tendency is to lie even when we have nothing to hide. Break that habit and make truth a part of your daily life.

Never distort nor cover up the truth again, even if you think a lie might help someone else. Lying certainly *didn't* help your mother. Of course, she is responsible for her actions. But will you take responsibility for your own?

Go to your mother and ask for her forgiveness as soon as possible. Tell her, 'Mother, I lied to you and I hurt you too. Will you forgive me?' Carefully think through what you are going to say before you talk to her. Don't make a long speech. Simply admit your wrongdoing and ask for her forgiveness. Then wait for her answer.

If your mother starts berating you and accusing you, listen to her for a while to see whether she calms down. You might say one more time, 'Mother, you are right, I was wrong. Will you please forgive me?'

Once you've asked for your mother's forgiveness, you've done your part. If she forgives you, well and good. If she won't, then lay the matter to rest for ever. It's *her* problem now. But you will be able to sleep in peace again knowing you've done the right thing. Write to me again, will you? I want to help you in any way I can.

17

Question: *Mr. Palau, my problem is alcoholism. I've tried to free myself but I've found it impossible. What can I do?*

You have written to me because you want to be free from the grip of alcohol. You're not alone. I have met alcoholics all over the world who want to be free – and try desperately – but they can't seem to manage it.

It is no secret that alcoholism is one of the greatest social problems we face today. About five times the entire population of the Falkland Islands – some 10,000 people – die every year in Britain because of alcoholism. According to government statistics, many hundreds of thousands more suffer from its adverse effects. Postmortems also show that 45 per cent. of the under-25s killed in road accidents died while intoxicated. As you and I both know, alcoholism is a serious problem.

Why does a person become an alcoholic? Usually it is because they are either looking for thrills, happiness and satisfaction, or looking for an escape from boredom, guilt or loneliness. Whatever the reason, they believe the lie that a drink can solve their problems. It only creates more!

What is alcoholism, anyway? We agree it is a problem. Many sociologists, psychologists and psychiatrists explain that alcoholism is a disease. Now that's a nice and proper and inoffensive way to talk about this problem. But they're wrong. Psychologist

Rex Julian Beaber aptly pointed out in the April 4, 1983, issue of *Newsweek* that our 'lust for scientific-sounding explanations is completely out of control . . . Ultimately we must assume responsibility for our actions.'

Alcoholism certainly produces many different diseases, but we cannot excuse it as if it were one. 'The acts of the sinful nature are obvious: sexual immorality, impurity and debauchery; idolatry and witchcraft; hatred, discord, jealousy, fits of rage, selfish ambition, dissensions, factions and envy; *drunkenness*, orgies, and the like' (Gal. 5: 19–21). Scripture clearly defines drunkenness as *sin*.

But that's insulting, you may say to yourself. No, on the contrary, the sooner we acknowledge our wrongdoing, the sooner we can find forgiveness and help from God and others.

I know of a number of men and women who have tried to excuse their alcoholism while inwardly crying for release from its tyranny. But it wasn't until they admitted their sinfulness and helplessness to overcome the bottle, and committed their life to Christ, that God completely liberated them from alcohol. They've never touched another drink since.

Christ can totally revolutionise your life. He can set you free from alcohol and truly meet your deepest needs. We read, 'Therefore, if anyone is in Christ, he is a new creation; the old has gone, the new has come!' (2 Cor. 5: 17). You have taken the first step by admitting your helplessness to overcome alcohol. Now turn to Christ and become a new creation in Him today.

18

Question: Mr. Palau, I discovered that my wife has been unfaithful to me. We have three children. I'm a very busy man with many commitments.

I noticed that my wife began having many activities outside our home, but never in the world thought I'd see her with another man. When I checked that she really had been unfaithful to me, it totally destroyed me.

I don't know what to do. I'm thinking about separation or divorce, but I love my children and know that our separation would be very difficult for them. What should I do?

You say you feel 'totally destroyed' by your wife's unfaithfulness, and I can see why. After all, every young man and woman dream of marrying that one special person and sharing their life together until death eventually separates them. To see that dream shattered later in life when you already have a family is certainly devastating.

When you and your wife joined your lives together in marriage, you became one. Her infidelity is tearing at that union and causing untold grief. No wonder the Bible says, 'Marriage should be honoured by all, and the marriage bed kept pure, for God will judge the adulterer and all the sexually immoral' (Heb. 13: 4).

Marital unfaithfulness is immoral. It's *sin*.

No matter what people say today, sin hurts. It's hurting you and your three children. It's also hurting your wife. Anybody can sin, but nobody can sin without suffering the consequences and hurting others in the process.

By nature everyone has a bent towards sin. Let's face it, we live in a fallen world as members of the fallen human race. Ever since Adam and Eve found themselves naked under the Tree of the Knowledge of Good and Evil, we have duplicated their rebellion against God's will in a thousand different ways. The Bible says, 'There is no one righteous, not even one' (Rom. 3:10).

But let's get down to the details. Why has your wife been drawn to and attracted and tempted by another man? Didn't you realise that your wife was growing cold towards you? You say in your letter, 'I am a very busy man and have many commitments.' That is no excuse – it may be the very root of your marital problems. You have been too busy to satisfy your wife's needs.

Now, don't misunderstand me. I'm not justifying your wife's actions. Nor am I blaming you for her immorality. She is responsible for her own moral choices. But you are responsible for yours. Your decision to invest more time and energy into your work than into your marriage was wrong.

You may be thinking, 'Luis, if I didn't work so hard, we wouldn't have what we need.' I'll tell you, it's better to have a happy home than a fancy one. It's better to have a faithful wife than one who has everything she wants – except your affection and leadership.

Apparently you are a leader in your profession and in your community, since so many commitments occupy your time. But are you a leader in your own home? Do you know what it means to be the head of your family? Now I'm talking pretty straightforwardly to you, because it was you who wrote to me and not your wife.

Serving as the head of your home does not mean

acting like a dictator or getting your own way all the time or having special privileges. Headship means fulfilling your responsibilities as a husband to guide in your family's decision-making process, to become accountable for the decisions that are made, to love your wife sacrificially, to be the strong leader she wants and needs.

God made man to be the strong side of the family. In the New Testament we read, 'Husbands... be considerate as you live with your wives, and treat them with respect as the weaker partner' (1 Pet. 3: 7). Now stronger doesn't mean superior. Weaker doesn't mean inferior. But the husband is ordained by God to care for his wife, protect her and love her. Is that the kind of husband you have been?

You and your wife have both made mistakes. Now you must make a choice. Will you tear your marriage in half by getting a divorce or rebuild it by seeking reconciliation?

I commend you for your concern about your children's welfare. You say, 'I love my children and know that our separation would be very difficult for them.' You're absolutely right!

A recently completed research project analysed the effects of divorce on 131 children over a ten-year period. The results? More than one third of the children were found to be 'consciously and intensely unhappy and dissatisfied with their life in the post-divorce family.' Another 29 per cent. still struggled with periods of unhappiness because they could not accept their parents' divorce. Even many of the children who were 'coping' still felt lonely and upset, and after a decade retained vivid memories of the fragmentation of their home.

Diana left three children – then aged 6, 5 and 1½ – in 1977 and moved to London. She explained her decision in the *Sunday Mirror:* 'If I had stayed I would have ended up embittered, telling them all their lives that I stayed just for them. Leaving nearly broke my heart but in the end I had to put *my needs first*.'

Stephen Rourke, executive director of a national organisation that works with troubled young people, has found the attitude expressed by Diana prevalent among the divorced. He says: 'It has become fashionable for parents to think of themselves first. They separate, and don't consider the children's needs. Taking care of "me" is their first priority.'

So again, I commend you for caring about your children's future, not just your own. From reading your letter, I sense that your children probably don't know about your wife's unfaithfulness. I wouldn't recommend telling them about it – now or later. They don't need to know about your failures, either, especially if they are young.

What is important now is your life-style in front of your children. They need to see you speaking gently, tenderly, forgivingly and patiently with your wife as a lover seeking reconciliation with his lover.

You may say, 'Luis, my wife has walked out on me and is seeing another man. How am I supposed to become reconciled to her?' Well, I can't offer you any *easy* answers, but I will give you several that will work.

First, actively invest more of your time and energy into fulfilling your responsibilities as a husband and father. Your work and other commitments must be curtailed and take less priority than your own wife and children.

Second, forgive your wife before you think again about divorcing her. Now that's not natural. It will go against everything you're probably feeling. But do it anyway. Consciously decide before God to forgive her for acting unfaithfully towards you.

Third, go and apologise to your wife for your failure to meet her needs and ask for her forgiveness. She may refuse to forgive you. But your responsibility is to confess your misplaced priorities to her. Perhaps she will forgive you and confess her own wrongdoing and ask for your forgiveness as well, so that together you both can work to rebuild your marriage. It is your responsibility to forgive your wife if and when she asks.

Fourth, confess your shortcomings to God and receive forgiveness through His Son, Jesus Christ. We haven't all committed immorality, though many have thought about it. But we've all sinned. Acknowledge your own unfaithfulness to God.

God is awesome, holy and just. He is also loving and compassionate. Because He loves us so much, He actually became a man in the person of Jesus of Nazareth. He loved us so much that He allowed Himself to die on a cross in order to pay the penalty for our sins.

Though we deserve the worst, Christ died in our place and now offers us the best: new, eternal life. God is offering you complete forgiveness and a new identity as one of His own. Will you accept His free gift of new life?

The most important step you can take to rebuild your marriage is to commit your life to Christ today. God says to you right now: 'That if you confess with your mouth, "Jesus is Lord," and believe in your heart that God raised him from the dead, you will be saved. For it is with your heart that you believe and are justified, and it is with your mouth that you confess and are saved' (Rom. 10: 9–10).

Dear Reader: Whatever your own situation may be, perhaps you, too, have never experienced God's forgiveness and become a new creation in Him. If the prayer below expresses the desire of your heart, use it as a guide to talk to God – silently if you wish – right now.

Dear God, I agree that I am a sinner. I have failed others – and most importantly, I have sinned against You.

Thank You for sending Your Son, Jesus Christ, to die on the Cross to take away my sins and to give me new life. Jesus, now You're alive and only You can make my marriage and family something beautiful. I commit myself to You. Thank You for giving me new hope today. Amen.

19

Question: *My fiancé and I have been going out together for seven years, but several months ago I found out he's been going with a married woman who has children. When her husband leaves for work, my fiancé goes to her house. I even saw him there once myself, but I didn't think it would turn into anything serious or lasting.*

But now I can tell he has become more and more distant towards me, not like before. Do you have some advice for him? What can I do? Should I let him go his own way or fight to get him back from that terrible, perverse woman?

I can't give you advice for your fiancé because he didn't ask for it. You wrote to me, not your fiancé. But I do have several observations and suggestions for you.

First, going out together for seven years is much too long. It's unnatural to be engaged and pretend you're going to get married, but keep putting it off. Apparently your fiancé started feeling bored and gave in to sexual temptations as a result.

Second, although you call your fiancé's mistress a 'terrible, perverse woman', he is no less guilty. Whether he became intimate with her once or a dozen times, he has committed sexual immorality. The Bible explains the serious implications of this sin: 'Flee from sexual immorality. All other sins a man commits are outside his body, but he who sins sexually sins against his own body' (1 Cor. 6: 18).

Third, a person like your fiancé who acts unfaithfully *before* marriage generally will also act unfaithfully *after* the wedding. Rarely does a person change his life-style unless a radical change takes place in his beliefs and convictions. Don't believe your fiancé if he promises to turn over a new leaf. What he needs is new life – new life in Jesus Christ.

So what should you do about your fiancé's unfaithfulness to you? After forgiving him in your heart, you must confront him and tell him what you have found out. Then tell him that you cannot approve of it and that you don't want to see him again. If he refuses to respect your request, ask your father (or perhaps an older brother) to tell him your relationship is finished.

Ending your engagement may be the hardest thing you'll ever do, humanly speaking. But why jeopardise your future by marrying an unfaithful man who may not even love you? That would only cause more heartache in the long run.

After ending your engagement, you may feel lonely and empty inside. That's understandable. But don't become involved in another serious relationship immediately in order to fill that void. Instead, look to your family, friends and God for support. They will be able to supply the balm of love and encouragement you need so as to heal emotionally.

Then trust God to bring the right type of young man into your life. Someone who loves God and will love you, care for you and remain faithful to you. The Bible says, 'Delight yourself in the Lord and he will give you the desires of your heart' (Ps. 37: 4). Why settle for less?

20

Question: *Luis, I am terribly bored with my job. I've been working at the same business for eight years. Almost every day I do the same type of work and I am bored with it and with life in general. I don't even know what to do with myself. I am single, 25 years old and I can't stand it any more. I feel I am choking to death. Have you been in this state yourself, Luis? What advice would you give me?*

Do you realise how fortunate you are even to have a job? Millions of people in Britain today would gladly work if they had your job. So thank God for that. But I agree with you that work can be boring.

Yes, I've been in your state. I used to work for the Bank of London in Argentina. Even though I was rising in position within the bank – partly because I spoke both English and Spanish – I felt bored stiff with the routine of my job. Let me recommend to you what I did to overcome that listless feeling.

First, get a loose-leaf notebook and begin to write down your goals in life. At 25 years of age, you certainly ought to have more important goals than just working eight hours a day. Work is fine. Without it you would become even more bored. But you need to consider in prayer God's will for your life.

To get started, try this exercise. Sit down and spend a long time thinking and praying about the goals you believe God would have you accomplish in your lifetime. Then write them down in your notebook. Don't try to do it in half an hour. Work on this for a week or two or more. Next, determine what you must do and what you must give in order to achieve those goals.

Perhaps you've never done this before, but I want to emphasise the talking to God about your goals. He doesn't want us to live life half-heartedly. Jesus Christ said, 'I have come that they may have life, and have it to the full' (John 10: 10). If you walk according to God's will for your life – as revealed in the Bible – you will never experience boredom again! He has exciting plans for you.

Personalise this promise: '"I know the plans I have for you," declares the Lord, "plans to prosper you and not to harm you, plans to give you hope and a future. Then you will call upon me and come and pray to me, and I will listen to you. You will seek me and find me when you seek me with all your heart"' (Jer. 29: 11–13).

So write down your goals, seeking the Lord and His plans for your life, and then contact me again. I want to hear from you.

21

Question: *Some people say that they are going to heaven when they die. Even though we all hope to go to heaven, I don't think anyone really knows for certain what will happen to them when they die. What do you think?*

American satirist Mark Twain claimed: 'People cannot stand much church. They draw the line at Sunday, once a week, and they do not look forward to it. But consider what heaven holds: church that lasts for ever! And they long for it, dream about it, and think they are going to be happy and enjoy it.'

Is *that* what heaven is like?

Or is heaven full of harps, pink clouds and chubby-cheeked cherubs? Is it angelic choirs, sombre faces and majestic boredom?

Such images are a gross caricature of God's dwelling-place. It was Paul Little who accurately described heaven as 'a dynamic, expanding, creative experience far beyond anything our finite minds can now comprehend'. The most significant aspect of heaven will not be the streets of gold but the fact that God is in dynamic fellowship with men. I want to be *there*!

A 93-year-old woman wrote to our office recently and said, 'If you do not hear from me again, it may be because I have gone to be with the Lord!' Isn't that beautiful? Death did not haunt her because she was sure of heaven. Such an assurance not only gives us a hope for the future, but a reason to live in the here and now. 'To believe in heaven is not to run away from life; it is to run towards it.'

When we die, we leave behind everything we *have* and take with us all we *are*. Jesus Christ has assured those who are His followers: 'My sheep listen to my voice; I know them, and they follow me. I give them eternal life, and they shall never perish; no one can snatch them out of my hand' (John 10: 27–8).

Later, on the night before His crucifixion, Jesus told His disciples: 'Do not let your hearts be troubled. Trust in God; trust also in me. In my Father's house are many rooms; if it were not so, I would have told you. I am going there to prepare a place for you. And if I go and prepare a place for you, I will come back and take you to be with me that you also may be where I am' (John 14: 1–3).

Now those are fabulous promises. And that's part of what makes the Christian life so exciting. That's what gives us such tremendous hope in the face of potential economic collapse, death or world-wide war. We aren't a part of what William Simon calls 'the "now" generation which wants to make it through the night and let the devil take care of tomorrow.' Our lives are guided by a perspective that encompasses all of eternity.

But promises are worthless unless you know they will be fulfilled, and then claim them. There is no question that God will do His part. But do you have 'a faith and knowledge resting on the hope of eternal life, which God, who does not lie, promised before the beginning of time' (Titus 1: 2)? Are you a follower and disciple of Christ? Have you staked your life and destiny on His Word? If not, make sure of heaven by trusting in Jesus Christ and committing your life to Him. Chapter 29 explains how you can make that decision today.

22

Question: *I would like you to give me advice on how I can overcome temptation in the area of sex. My husband is overseas. He has been gone now for nine months and will be gone for seven more. I'm very lonely and I desire affection and love. Please help me.*

Thousands of men and women struggle with the same temptations that you do. Whether because of military service, separation, divorce, illness or work, many married people find themselves alone from time to time. In your case, you have been apart from your spouse for an exceptionally long period.

You desire affection and love *now*, even though your husband won't be home for several months. Your desire is intense because we *need* companionship and closeness. But sexual intimacy isn't the only way to try to meet that need.

Having said that, I want to emphasise that sex is good. It is a gift from God (Gen. 2: 24). Some of us came from backgrounds that treated sex and sexual desires as evil. Of course, that is the opposite of what the Bible teaches. After all, God created our capacity as humans to enjoy sexual intimacy and intercourse. Having created our first parents, God officiated at their union and called it 'very good'.

Sex becomes ugly, however, whenever it is misused. When you are tempted to satisfy your need for affection and love by becoming sexually involved with a man other than your husband, you are being enticed to misuse the God-given gift of sex. Yielding to such a temptation would be disastrous.

Several months ago a friend of mine – a fine, happy, outgoing gentleman – ruined his life and destroyed his marriage by becoming involved in sexual immorality. He has left his wife and children for another woman and today he is the most miserable person I've ever seen. Why? Not because anybody is pointing a finger at him, but because he's living in defiance of God's commandments.

When God said, 'You shall not commit adultery' (Exod. 20: 14), He didn't intend to kill our happiness. He strongly desired to safeguard it! Yet sexual immorality is becoming more commonplace every day – and so are the bitter results.

Our culture's obsession with sex has occurred, in part, because we've equated physical contact with affection and love. Amid the graffiti scrawled on a wall at the airport near my home are the words, 'Love is sex'. That's false! Even George Leonard, a veteran of the sexual revolution and author of *The End of Sex* (published in 1983), admits that one of the movement's 'wrong turns' was to assume intercourse and intimacy were synonymous. They're not.

The Bible clearly teaches and experience proves that sex becomes a meaningful expression of love only within the marriage relationship. Since your husband will be gone for another seven months, you need to take several positive steps of action to resist sexual temptation.

First, ask God to help you control your thoughts and desires. Wrong thoughts lead to wrong actions. Although it's impossible to prevent wrong thoughts from entering our minds, we are responsible for how long they linger there. When they come, dismiss them at once by God's strength. Then heed this wise precept, 'whatever is true, whatever is noble, whatever is right, whatever is pure, whatever is lovely, whatever is admirable – if anything is excellent or praiseworthy – think about such things' (Phil. 4: 8). If you protect your thoughts, you'll guard your affections as well.

Second, maintain open lines of communication with your husband. Write to him regularly and ring him occasionally, if possible. Surprise him with a box of gifts to remind him how much you love him. Use your imagination to let your husband know you're still in love with *him*!

Third, set specific goals to accomplish during the next seven months. Channel your energy into completing projects around the house and doing other things you've wanted to do – some day. Don't waste these valuable months!

Fourth, make a commitment to your local church (Heb. 10: 24–5). Channel some of your energy into getting more involved in God's work.

Finally, develop close friendships with other women in your area. Perhaps you know several other women whose husbands travel from time to time. Such friends – especially good Christian friends – will be able to encourage you and support you in a special way until your husband returns.

23

Question: *About four years ago my mum and dad split up. I stayed with Dad, and my two sisters and Mum went to live with another man. My dad was hurt, angry and unhappy. All my own dreams for a happy family, for love, for trust, were shattered. I've hated my mum. I just can't forgive her. Don't I have the right to feel angry and hurt? Yes or no?*

Every boy and girl has the right to grow up in a stable, loving home. That's why God formed the institution of marriage and the family. He holds parents (or guardians) responsible to care and provide for each child.

Your rights as a young man have been violated. Your mother has acted irresponsibly by walking out on you and your father. She has slapped your father in the face and left you crying inside. No one can go through such an experience and not be deeply affected emotionally.

So yes, you have a right at first to feel angry and hurt because your mother split your home. But you must deal biblically with these emotions. You have a right to feel upset because she's ignored your needs. Your feelings of anger are normal. It's a cause-and-effect response.

Anger is our natural, right response to discovering the ugly side of life. As a teenager, you have already discovered that we live in a world that can be extremely wicked, selfish and cruel. The very foundations of our society – including the family – are crumbling. When your own family shattered, so did your dreams. But even though you can't change what's happened, don't lose hope for the future.

Don't give up your dreams for a happy family. *You* can have a fantastic marriage – if you build it on the right foundation. And that foundation isn't your parents. (You've learned that.) It isn't the perfect girl. (You'll never find her.) Let God be the solid rock on which you stand. Storms will come, of course, but He will make your marriage last (Matt. 7: 24-7).

And don't give up your dreams for love and trust. I realise your mother betrayed you. You've learned that others may fail you. But don't fail them. Without love and trust, life becomes mere existence. So take the risk to give to others in love, and befriend them in trust. And remember that God is worthy of your complete trust. He loved you so much that He gave His very life for you. His death on the cross expresses the highest degree of love ever shown: 'Greater love has no one than this, that one lay down his life for his friends (John 15: 13). If God loved you that much even though He knows all about you, doesn't He deserve your love and trust in return?

Keep your dreams for the future alive by dealing with your anger God's way. No matter how angry you feel, you have no right to strike back at your mother physically or verbally. The Bible says: 'Do not take revenge, my friends, but leave room for God's wrath, for it is written: "It is mine to avenge; I will repay," says the Lord' (Rom. 12: 19).

Similarly, you must not remain angry. To be honest, it isn't worth the trouble to hate your mother. Unresolved anger probably won't change your mother, but it certainly will change you. It will embitter you and taint everything you do. That's why God commands, 'Do not let the sun go down while you are still angry' (Eph. 4: 26). How many times has the sun gone down since you became angry at your mother? Isn't it time to get rid of it for ever?

First, realise it's not going to be easy to forgive your mother. Everything inside you might be screaming, 'But she doesn't deserve it!' Do it anyway, for your own good at least. Do it because God says: 'Bear with each other and forgive whatever grievances you may have against one another. Forgive as the Lord forgave you' (Col. 3: 13).

Second, you must choose to forgive her completely now. 'But Luis,' you might be saying, 'I just can't.' Oh? You're really saying, 'I won't.' If you still feel you can't forgive your mother, I believe it is because you have never personally experienced what it is to be forgiven by God. In that case, you first need to settle matters with Him, and experience His forgiveness in your life.

24

Question: *My youngest sister died and it had a tremendous effect on our whole family, including me. Why did God allow her to die?*

In our daily experiences we often ask the question, 'Why?' No other question comes from our lips more often. Yet 'Why?' is the one question no one can completely answer. Why did God allow your sister to die? I cannot say.

I was only ten years old when death first struck my own family. My father died just hours before I returned home from a term at the British boarding-school I attended in Argentina. I had no way of knowing what had happened as I stepped off the train and ran home. But as I neared my house I could hear weeping.

My relatives tried to intercept me as I ran through the gate and up to the house; I brushed past them and was in the door before my mother even knew I was back. Tears filled my eyes when I saw my father's dead body lying in front of me.

I felt completely devastated by my father's death. My world seemed shattered and confusing. I was angry at everything and everyone. *It isn't fair*, I thought. *Why couldn't my dad die in old age like other dads?*

'Why?' All of us wrestle with that question at different times during our life. Only God knows why your sister died at such an early age. Perhaps God wanted to spare her from some future suffering of pain or injustice. But who am I to say? If God is God, how can I explain His ways?

God has declared, 'As the heavens are higher than the earth, so are my ways higher than your ways and my thoughts than your thoughts' (Isa. 55: 9). We cannot comprehend them.

In the New Testament we read that two of the apostles were imprisoned (Acts 12: 1–11). God miraculously delivered the apostle Peter; but allowed the apostle James to be killed. Why? The Bible doesn't say. Because God has all power and control, He could have prevented James's death. But for some reason He knew it was best not to intervene.

No one knows when the time of death will come, but most of us will admit its coming is certain. Longfellow succinctly observed, 'The young may die, and the old must.' The Bible also reminds us, 'Just as man is destined to die' (Heb. 9: 27).

Your sister's time to die came early. Your own time will come before you know it. Death *always* comes too soon. We were meant to enjoy eternity.

When death strikes, we sometimes shake our fist at God in despair. But that's an awful thing to do. God hates death more than you or I.

If you take your sister's death seriously, as you obviously have, then allow it to draw you closer to God and to His purposes for you. God does not want anyone to perish, but all to turn to Him and receive His offer of life everlasting. In the Bible we learn, 'the gift of God is eternal life in Christ Jesus our Lord' (Rom. 6: 23). Accept His gift today.

25

Question: *As for me, I really don't believe there is a God and I don't believe there isn't a God. I have no conviction either way. But I'm wondering if you'd help me because I have noticed that a lot of my friends are believing in the Lord and I don't know if it's right for me.*

Most people seem to feel the same way you do. You're not sure God exists, but you can't say dogmatically that He *doesn't* exist, either.

You're not an atheist because an atheist says he's absolutely sure there is no God. Such a person exercises a tremendous amount of faith in himself to make such a claim.

Someone has described an atheist as 'a man who looks through a telescope and tries to explain what he can't see'. That's why people laughed when the Russian cosmonauts announced that God didn't exist because they never saw Him in space.

Britain has had its share of well-known atheists who have ridiculed the idea of God, even though they couldn't offer conclusive proof against His existence. Atheists such as Bertrand Russell, W. Somerset Maugham and George Bernard Shaw come to mind.

But listen to Shaw's own testimony later in life: 'The science to which I pinned my faith is bankrupt... Its counsels which should have established the millennium have led directly to the suicide of Europe. I believed them once ... In their name I helped destroy Europe. I believed them once ... In their name I helped destroy the faith of millions of worshippers in the temples of a thousand creeds. And now they look at me and witness the tragedy of an atheist who has lost *his* faith' (*Too True to be Good*). Shaw the atheist became Shaw the agnostic.

An agnostic, like yourself, admits that he doesn't believe in God. Some try to ignore God, but deep inside they aren't 100-per-cent. sure He doesn't exist. And that uncertainty makes them feel uneasy.

Augustine, a philosopher, experienced those same feelings many years ago. Later in life he wrote in his *Confessions*, 'You made us for Yourself and our heart is restless until it rests in You.' He recognised the vacuum that exists within every man – an emptiness caused by man's basic tendency (however disguised or covered up or seemingly dignified) towards evil.

That subtle rebellion against his Creator leaves man restless and unsatisfied. Oh, for a moment you may experience thrills, but the restlessness always returns. That's why I believe you wrote to me. You said you want to know if believing in God would be right for you. Yes, it is!

God has revealed His existence and character to us in many ways. The majestic order and design of the universe speak of His infinite power and control. If the creation defies our comprehension, then certainly the Creator exceeds our explanation. As finite beings, we cannot understand God fully. (Otherwise, He wouldn't be God!) But He has revealed many specific things about Himself to us (Ps. 19: 1-6).

As you read the Bible – which I strongly urge you to do if you want to be intellectually honest – you will discover that the Lord reveals Himself as more than the Creator. He is also 'the compassionate and gracious God, slow to anger, abounding in love and faithfulness, maintaining love to thousands, and forgiving wickedness, rebellion and sin. Yet he does not leave the guilty unpunished' (Exod. 34: 6-7). And God is yet more.

God is the Creator, yes. But He is also the Holy One and the Gracious One. If God created us and demanded perfection – but wasn't gracious – there would be no hope for us. We would be banished from His presence to hell with no hope for reconciliation.

Yet the good news is this: God is very gracious. He has made a way of reconciliation through His Son, Jesus Christ. Christ suffered and bled and died on the Cross – and rose from the dead – to take the punishment *we* deserved. Now God seeks to reconcile us to Himself.

God wants you to know more than certain facts *about* Him. He wants you to know *Him*! And you can! Don't sit on the side-lines of life as an agnostic. Believe in God today and commit your life to Him. It's the only right thing you can do.

26

Question: *I am having a problem with my 19-year-old brother. He is caught up in one of the cult movements, and it has got to the point where he can't get along with anyone in the family.*

Some of the things he does – especially to his body and physical appearance – are really strange. He also works fourteen, sixteen, sometimes eighteen hours a day in a store that belongs to the cult. I just don't know how to get through to him!

Your problem is common today – too common – and I can understand your concern. It's shocking and frightening to watch a family member become engulfed in a cult group.

Because of the freedoms enjoyed in Britain, everyone has a right to choose the life they want to live as long as they don't break the basic laws of the land. We cherish that freedom, but with it comes the possibility that someone we love may join a cult.

Isn't it amazing that while people have so much trouble believing what *God* declares in the Bible, they will believe anything some *man* says? Intelligent men and women refuse to believe Jesus Christ's words, for example, when He said: 'I tell you the truth, everyone who sins is a slave of sin ... So if the Son sets you free, you will be free indeed' (John 8: 34, 36). But they will turn right round and believe the blatant lies uttered by a cult leader!

Satan is the master deceiver behind the cults and he is out to deceive mankind.

Jesus also said, 'the devil . . . was a murderer from the beginning, not holding to the truth, for there is no truth in him. When he lies, he speaks his native language, for he is a liar and the father of lies. Yet because I tell you the truth, you do not believe me!' (John 8: 44-5).

Many young people who join a cult eventually drop out, as your brother probably will. But they're never the same. The psychological manipulation practised by the various cults over a period of time can permanently affect an individual's personality. Tony Freeland described in the *Glasgow Herald* what often happens: 'These kids come out of the cults totally changed people. As my mother used to say about my brother, it was like having a living bereavement in the family. We got back the body, but we did not get back the mind.'

You express concern about your brother's 'strange' behaviour. But that's not the real problem. Rather, it's the spiritual deception and slavery under which he is struggling. Anyone who goes into one of the cults is looking for spiritual reality. They haven't found it in their family or elsewhere, so they turn to a cult. Tragically, they play right into the hands of those who promote spiritual *non*reality.

In your letter you also express your desire to help your brother to see what this cult is doing to him and to help him get out of it. What's the best way to do this?

I don't recommend 'deprogramming'. I admire those who want to use it to help a loved one caught in the snare of a cult. I realise that their concern and despair are great, but I think that deprogramming goes against the very freedoms we cherish and want our loved ones to enjoy again. Deprogramming can become as forceful and manipulative as the brainwashing tactics the cults themselves use.

The best way to help your brother is to model reality before him. If your brother sees the joy and transforming power of Christ in you, then he won't be able to help but realise, 'Hey, my sister has everything this cult promises but doesn't provide. I want what she has!'

Are you a real Christian? Have you committed your life to Christ? If so, then pray that God will break the power of Satan in your brother's life. Don't give up praying for him. Then when opportunities arise, select a verse of Scripture and quote it while speaking to him. Don't argue – simply reinforce that one verse in his thinking. Allow God to use you as a channel to liberate your brother.

27

Question: *I'm involved in spiritism. I'm not really far into it, but I've played games with it, as people call it. Anything I've done has been to help other people. I know I still have my faith in God, but I'm beginning to wonder if what I'm doing is right.*

I have discovered that many people, like yourself, are interested and active to some extent in spiritism, black magic and the occult. Researchers have found that eight out of every ten British young people have had some personal involvement with ouija, levitation, seances, horoscopes or palmistry.

I find it very interesting that, today, in spite of all our scientific progress, people are more than ever before turning to occultism. To me, it is the strangest thing that people will refuse to accept the virgin birth of Jesus Christ but they will believe in UFOs from other planets and they will become engrossed in parapsychology.

You wrote to me after seeking to help others by dabbling in such activities. Yet you say that something has made you wonder if what you are doing is right.

I commend you for seeking to serve others. But let me also warn you: If you don't avoid the occult completely, you will end up serving the desires of the king of darkness, Satan himself.

Some time ago I went with my boys to see the film, *Star Wars*. They insisted that I go with them. And I was intrigued that throughout the plot there was this idea of good versus evil.

Similarly, the Bible speaks about light and darkness, about right and wrong. And the Bible is very clear when it says that the world is divided into two camps: either God or the devil, either right or wrong, either light or darkness.

On the one side there is God. On the other side there is the 'god' of this world, Satan. Bob Dylan talks about this in his song, 'You've Gotta Serve Somebody'. You only have two choices. You can either serve the devil or the Lord, but everyone has to serve somebody. In this case, you are unwittingly serving Satan, even though you claim to believe in God. Remember, even the demons believe in God – and shudder (Jas. 2: 19).

It isn't enough to have faith in God, as you claim to have. You must commit your life to Christ, who came 'to destroy the devil's work' (1 John 3: 8). The Bible also says, 'Submit yourselves, then, to God. Resist the devil, and he will flee from you' (Jas. 4: 7). Then you will know God personally. Then you will be rescued from the dominion of darkness and brought into the kingdom of light (Col. 1: 12–13).

Once you commit your life to Christ, forsake anything to do with spiritism (Acts 19: 18–19). Instead, read the Bible and do what it says. In that way you will be cleansed and will walk in God's pure light.

28

Question: *I am single and I work in an important company. I receive a good salary, but in my frustration I have thought many times about suicide. Tell me, is it an unforgivable sin to consider suicide?*

You have everything the world has to offer. You're young and single. You have prestige and social standing. You have wealth and possessions. Others probably envy you and strive to obtain what you already enjoy. But for some reason you are churning inside.

You feel frustrated to the point where you want to take your own life. You've thought about it many times. Perhaps you've already planned how you will kill yourself, where you will do it and when. If so, my words are doubly urgent to you. But at least for the moment you feel hesitant to take that final step.

You've asked me to tell you whether considering suicide is an unforgivable sin. It seems as if you have had some religious instruction or influence in the past. Despite that training, you are still seriously considering ending your life. But you haven't even told me what is frustrating you.

Your frustration reminds me of the many men and women I have counselled over the years who have been contemplating suicide. Some have wrestled with unemployment, divorce or the death of a loved one. Others have despaired because of loneliness, bitterness or poor health. Whatever may be causing your frustration, you believe it's reason enough to end it all. But I challenge you to analyse where your urge to kill yourself is coming from.

Your desire to commit suicide is coming from the great enemy of our souls, I believe. We know him as the adversary, the devil. Jesus Christ also spoke of him as the father of lies, Satan himself. On one occasion Jesus called this enemy of ours a vicious thief: 'The thief [Satan] comes only to steal and kill and destroy' (John 10: 10). The Lord Jesus, however, could say, 'I have come that you may have life, and have it to the full' (John 10: 10). Satan wants to destroy you. But consider the implications of allowing him to seduce you to eternal doom.

Suicide is not the unforgivable sin that the Bible speaks of in Mark 3: 29. But suicide is a serious sin. And considering suicide is usually a symptom of an unforgiven heart.

You can experience God's forgiveness and receive new life in Him immediately by confessing your suicidal desires and committing your life to Him. When such great men as Moses, Elijah, Job and Jonah wanted to die during a particularly frustrating point in their lives, God forgave their sins and took away their destructive thoughts. In addition, God gave them purpose and fulfilment in life. God loves you and wants to do the same for you. I urge you to turn to Him today. You have nothing to lose, but everything God offers to gain.

The next chapter tells you how you can commit your life to Christ this very hour. Don't put this book down until you discover how to make that decision.

29

Question: *I'll be honest with you. I've tried living the Christian life as the Bible says, but it's too difficult for me. I'm tempted to stop trying. Do you have a suggestion?*

You say the Christian life is too difficult for you, but it really isn't. It's *impossible.* Apart from the power of the Lord Jesus Christ living within the hearts of people, no one can live the Christian life. In your own frustration, you say you're tempted to give up Christianity. You are obviously confused as to what it is to be a real Christian.

As I have talked to hundreds of people around the world, I have discovered that many people believe the following myths about what makes someone a Christian:

Myth 1: Believing in God makes you a Christian

Eight out of ten people in England say they believe there is a God. But are they all Christians? Colonel James Irwin, remembered for his Apollo 15 moon mission, told me that while in a Moslem country a Moslem leader said to him, 'You talk about God so much, why aren't you a Moslem?'

Do you see my point? If you can be a Moslem and believe in God, then it is not 'believing in God' that makes you a Christian!

Myth 2: Going to church makes you a Christian

People go to church all the time – for a multitude of reasons. But that doesn't make them Christians. Even some thieves go to church.

There are people who go to church because it's a social habit. Others go because their family makes them go.

It is true that Christians go to church. But it is not the church-going that makes a person a Christian.

Myth 3: Praying doesn't make you a Christian

Certainly, Christians pray. But just because you pray it doesn't mean you're a Christian. Hindus pray all the time. Moslems pray five times a day.

The late President Sadat of Egypt, when travelling abroad, carried a little rug to kneel down on five times daily to pray to Mohammed.

So, praying doesn't make someone a Christian.

Myth 4: Living a good life makes you a Christian

Put alongside the Yorkshire Ripper you may feel that you are ready for sainthood. Even compared with your family and friends you may think yourself a paragon. But God's standard of goodness is very different. He puts you up against His Son, Jesus Christ, who was absolutely perfect. Compared with this level of perfection our own goodness looks pretty shoddy.

Remember, there have always been plenty of 'good' people in the world. So if goodness was enough, God need not have sent Jesus. The fact that Jesus had to come to die on the Cross to make our forgiveness possible shows that goodness does not make someone a Christian.

Myth 5: Reading the Bible makes you a Christian

Of course Christians love the Bible. Some of us read it daily. But just reading the Bible doesn't mean that you are a Christian.

When Karl Marx was 15 he wrote a fantastic explanation of the meaning of part of John's Gospel. Great theologians agree with what he said. But Karl Marx, although he read the Bible, never claimed to be a Christian.

Read the Bible all you can. But remember, doing so won't make you a Christian.

Myth 6: Talking about Jesus Christ makes you a Christian

Many people talk about Jesus Christ and even speak well of Him. They may be teachers, ministers or church leaders, for example. But they may not even believe that what the Bible says about Jesus is true. They may be talking about a Jesus that fits into their way of thinking, rather than the Jesus of history and the Bible.

Myth 7: You can be born a Christian

I've met people who have told me, 'I was born in a Christian country so of course I am a Christian. What else could I be?'

The answer is that they could be a lot of things.

Someone may be born in a stable. But that doesn't make them a horse. Nor does being born in an airport make someone an aeroplane.

Now let me tell you how you can become a real Christian right now as you finish reading this book.

97

Fact 1: Admit that your sins have separated you from God

How does a man or a woman become a Christian? The Bible teaches first that you must admit that your sins keep you separated from God. Have you ever owned up to God about those things in your life that hurt Him? Selfishness, pride, greed, immorality and the rest?

The Bible says, 'for all have sinned and fall short of the glory of God' (Rom. 3: 23). You know that includes you – and that it is time to own up to God and to receive the forgiveness that He wants to give you.

Fact 2: Believe the miracle of the Cross

Second, you must believe what Christ has done for you on the Cross. The Bible says, 'Christ died for sins' (1 Pet. 3: 18).

When Jesus died on the Cross, it was so that each one of us could be forgiven. We deserve to be punished for the wrong that we have done in God's eyes. But God sent His Son to take our punishment on His shoulders on the Cross.

It is like a judge finding a prisoner guilty and then stepping into the dock to receive the sentence himself. What magnificent love!

You may not completely understand how it is possible for God to place the penalty for your sin on His Son. But you do not need to understand everything all at once. You need only to believe that it is true.

Nobody understands electricity. Did you know that? Scientists talk about it as a fundamental property of all matter. They can create electrical charges and harness electricity, but, as a Stanford University scientist once told me, 'Electricity in its essence is quite unexplainable.'

When you become a real Christian, you may not understand it all at the beginning. But as you read the

Bible and allow God to teach you, your understanding will grow.

Fact 3: You must receive Christ for yourself

The final step you must take is to receive Christ for yourself. You cannot inherit faith. God doesn't have any grandchildren.

Don't say, 'My father was a fine Christian and I was brought up in a fine Christian home.' That will not make you one of God's children.

Experience Christ for yourself. All of us who belong to Christ had to come for ourselves. Have you come to Him yet? Have you ever made that decision?

The Bible says, 'Yet to all who received him, to those who believed in his name, he gave the right to become children of God' (John 1: 12).

You ask, 'How?' The best way I know is simply to bow your head in prayer, own up about your sins to God, by faith open your heart to Christ, believe in Him and receive Him.

Pray this prayer:

Heavenly Father, I want to be a real Christian. I realise that my sins have separated me from You. Please forgive me. I believe in what Christ did for me on the Cross. I don't completely understand it, but I accept it by faith. I do want Christ in my heart. I want to have eternal life. I want to be a child of Yours. Please come into my life, Lord Jesus, and make me Your child right now. I'll follow you and obey You for ever. Amen.

If you prayed that prayer in faith to God, you now belong to Him and you will want to get to know Him better. The best way is to read the Bible. Start with the Gospel of Luke and read it like a novel. But remember that this is God's way of speaking to us. As you read, look for examples to follow or instructions to obey.

Saturate yourself with the Bible. Your thought patterns and emotions will begin to change as you read the Word of God.

Second, meet with other Christians. Find a church where the Bible is explained, where the Gospel is proclaimed, where the minister believes the Bible is God's Word. Go to church, talk to the minister. Say, 'I received Christ,' and see what happens. If the minister doesn't seem interested in helping you to grow spiritually, then find some church that can help you.

Third, begin to pray. You talked to the Lord just now. He answered your prayer. He loves you, He's your Father. Communication is the key to any relationship. Your relationship with God can only grow as you talk to Him in prayer.

If you have committed your life to God, write to me so that I can rejoice with you in that most important of all decisions. I want to send you some helpful literature and try to answer any other questions you may have.

YOUR TURN

Have I left any questions unanswered in this book that concern you? If so, please feel free to contact me so that I can answer *your* questions. Write to the office nearest to you.

In Europe: 112 City Road, London EC1V 2NB, England.

In Canada: P.O. Box 158, White Rock, B.C. V4B 5C6.

In the United States: P.O. Box 1173, Portland, OR 97207.

I want to hear from you!

INDEX

SUBJECTS DISCUSSED IN THIS BOOK: